A Dream without A Song

(Faith or Fear)

CW00472298

A Dream without A Song

(Faith or Fear)

Publishing Inc.
Lonnie C Edwards Jr.

Email: nlt52@live.com

COPYWRITE © 2010 Lonnie C Edwards Jr.

Edited by: Lucretia Thurman

Cover by: Lonnie C Edwards Jr.

Written By Lonnie C Edwards Jr.

This book is dedicated to every couple that has had a hard time believing in each other or believing in the will of God. I would like to say, God will work out all your problems if you keep him in your life, No matter how bad it looks he will work out the best life for you. I would also like to say, that this book is not written to hurt anyone's feelings, but to teach people how to get better with themselves and learn how to put God first.

This book is about how I found true love in God and became stronger through my mental, physical, and emotional pains. It also shows you the reader how if you don't keep God in your marriage or life that you and your spouse will live in unforgivable fears. The title A Dream without A Song (Faith or Fear) means that your life is your dream and what you want out of life is your song. For example a women is doing her best in her marriage/life, but she is beaten by her husband daily and her cry/ tears becomes her song because it is what she is getting out of life not what she is wanting out of life, although she is displaying faith through her marriage she is living in fear during her marriage. This is a small example of how we need to learn what real love is and let God lead us in our walk with him. I also want to add some points such as forgiveness and love on a real unconditional level by asking the big question.

What is real love, everyone wants to know, but no one wants to learn. God teaches us to love our neighbor as we would love ourselves and to love unconditionally. In Mark chapter 11 verse 25 Jesus said" when you stand praying, if you hold anything against anyone, forgive him or her, so our Father in Heaven may forgive you of your sins". Also in Colossians chapter 3 verse 13 said" forgive whatever grievances that you may have against one another, Forgive as the Lord forgave you". I believe true love is to honor the love that God wants us to have for each other. As I said before everyone wants real love, but know one wants to work for it or believe in it. I believe one of the main reasons that our marriages don't work is, we fail to work on the six things that God hates such as; a proud look, a lying tongue, hands that shed innocent blood, a heart that devises wicked imagination, feet that are swift in running to mischief, a false witness that speaks lies, and he that sows discord among brethren. Proverbs chapter 6 verses 16-19.

We have so much pride and unforgivable love in our hearts leaving us with no room for believing in real love. Everyone has done wrong, the problem is no one believes they were wrong in the relationship therefore; we don't forgive each other in our relationship, leaving us without trust or love for the future. Now don't get me wrong if you have done everything humanly and spiritually possible and you were in a very abusive relationship whether it is mental, physical, emotional, spiritual or sexual. Yes I said sexual, people just don't realize how important a healthy sex life is, but I will get in to that later in the book.

Table of Contents

Chapter 1
The Crush (love and mob life)

It all started when my mother and father split up and we moved from Peoria, Illinois to Little Rock, Arkansas. This move was really hard on me, but the best thing that happened to me out of this move was I met the love of my life at Hall High School which was the school that my brother and I had to attend after moving to Little Rock. There was a girl that I felt was so pretty to me, but me being that guy that I am I wasn't going to sweat her, I was just too cool for that, besides I had just moved down here and didn't know anyone at that school but my cousin on my mother's side.

I checked her out for a while, but I never tried talking with her due to not knowing if she would talk to me or if she had a boyfriend. One day out the blue I was walking down the hall and felt a hand on my butt, then I looked to my right and saw this pretty girl that I had been checking out walking next to me with her hand on my butt, I guess she was checking me out too, but who knew. She was like a light down from Heaven, her eyes were like stars and her lips looked softer then feathers from a dove. I knew when I first saw her that I had to make her my girlfriend and as time went by, we began to date and hangout. We hung out at my aunt's house quite often, checking out movies, playing games with each other. We also talked on the phone daily which made us want to be around each other more and more. She knew that my mother needed to find another place to live so she started to help us look for a house to live in, because we needed to have our own space and moving out of my aunt's house was a must.

I was having the time of my life, being with her made me feel so cool inside. We continued to date and I then knew there was a God out there who loved me and allowed me to have someone as lovely as my girlfriend. It was fun and yes we had some ups and we had some downs, for example when it came time for my prom we broke up for a little bit and I talked with a another girl just to make her mad something that young fools do, but I was sorry for doing that and I knew it was not the right thing to do. I didn't know what made us go apart from each other, but it didn't last, she and I couldn't be away from each other long. We had a lot of fun together and I felt no one could keep us from seeing each other. I believed what we had was real, not thinking about how young we were. I did end up taking her to my prom and it really made me feel good to have her with me. It was a night to remember, life for me was pretty cool, but I did have a baby on the way, something that occurred when I first moved to Arkansas and it was previous to meeting my girlfriend. I was just a friend to the young lady, but I was not going to be just like all the other men who didn't like taking care of their responsibility. I let the young lady know that I would take care of my son when he is born. I didn't let it get me down and I felt like I could make my girlfriend happy no matter what, even though I was a young man with a baby on the way.

Time went by and the end of the year was coming I was about to graduate from high school. I really didn't know what I wanted to do with my life, so I felt that when I graduated from high school I should go back to Peoria, Illinois. She was cool with that besides she had another year to go in high school herself. The time came, I graduated from high school and it was time for me to head back home to Peoria, Illinois. Now part of me left because I felt that I was not letting her live her life by being so young and in love, but what did I know I was just a kid myself.

After I graduated I went back to Peoria, Illinois not knowing the life that I was about to

become involved with or what kind of trouble was headed my way.   Thank God I made

it to Peoria safely and soon as I got there I hooked up with my older brother whom I

looked up to, because that's what little brothers do. We began hanging out and soon after

that I chose to involve myself with the GD's aka the Gangster Disciples or now (Growth

and Development).

Now this is an organization that was well known for taking care of their business

and by me being young with no life I felt it would be a cool thing for me to do and its

always cool to be a part of a family, so why not be part of this one? They showed me love

and had my back on any type of problem that I faced. Now I do have a family, but it felt

different and I knew that my older brother was there and disrespecting us was not an

option. Now this organization is like a job, for example there are many position that you

can be appointed for such as (COS) chief of security, but in order to get it you have to be

chosen for it. Now I had a position that I was chosen for, but I did not start off with it. We

hung out a lot at the Bottom Line which was a big money spot for us. One day we were

hanging outside of it and a problem had occurred and the region of the north side wanted

us to step up to handle it, which at that time we were happy to do so, but my older brother

knew that we were fresh and just got back from Arkansas, he let them know that he didn't

want my brother and I to be involved with something that would come back on us when

we got older. My brothers Bozo, Giggles, Flame, and I watched each others back inside

of the Mob and I thank God for them because we made our presence known when we

hung out. One of my jobs in the organization was to be security for the bosses when they hung out at clubs or pulling security on money spots, yes we got paid for beating up crack heads that got out of hand. Now I must say one thing about pulling security you had to be alert at all times, not hanging with girls, not wearing sandals on your feet and being ready for whatever goes down, even if it may cost you your life. This mob life goes by very fast, but it gets old and I was starting to miss my girlfriend even though we hadn't been talking as much, she did send me a picture of her and my son whom she had been helping take care of after he was born and that made me really miss them. But living this fast life doesn't allow you to have any time to focus on anything outside of the mob not even Arkansas. The sad part was I was too focused on the Mob at the time. We did so much in so little time, but all good things must come to an end, now keep in mind I still continued to pray because I knew that the only one that was going to keep us out of real trouble was God so I prayed all the time even when doing wrong. Now living this life gives you no security for the future and something is always going to put you to the test, such as hanging out at a club called Stingers, we always carried guns when we hung out and I really didn't like doing that but sometimes in this life you don't really have a choice.

For example, one night we were just hanging out at Stingers night club doing what we usually do to have fun, not knowing that the altercation that occurred last week was going to start off a war with the Gangster Disciples and the Black Disciples known as the (BD) who was another strong organization in the state of Illinois, they too were known for taking care of their business as well as the Gangster Disciples. Giggles and I were out on the side of the club talking, when we noticed about 20 Black Disciples marching down the street headed toward Stingers, they were marching like they were ready for war.

Giggles had the gun and was supposed to fire on them before they made it to the club's parking lot, he tried, but the gun jammed so he was unable to do so, then all hell broke out, there were people running, shooting, fighting all around us and God still let us remain safe and unharmed, in the midst of danger. After this event there was a series of out breaks around town, the organization was on full alert. I was appointed personal security to one of the organizational leaders; they were not to travel alone. So now I'm thinking "Wow, I'm back in Peoria, Illinois and I don't know why, but what I did know was that I missed my girlfriend and my new son." I know, I'm really deeply involved with the mob now and leaving was not an option at this time, although I chose to stay in Peoria, I still tried not to think about Arkansas or even try to bring this lifestyle back to Arkansas I tell you people this was not a really fun time at all, for example, like watching your back, or carrying guns with you at all time, it's like feeling death in the wind. It's like every time I got in trouble or we got shot at I thought about getting back to my girl and making a new life with her. After a while of the mob life I noticed that it was getting old and the only thing out there for me was death or jail. So yes, my passion for her love grew more and more, then it happened, I saw death in the mob life one last time. It was a calm day, Giggles and I were hanging out in the front of our spot, now the spot was where about six or seven soldiers lived and it was clean, with big screen TVs, nice furniture, fish tank as long as the wall filled with my favorite fish, Piranhas. Now that might not be much, but to a young soldier such as myself it was the way of life. Now back to the story, Giggles and I noticed one BD drove past the spot really fast, I knew Giggles was strapped and my gun was in the house so I told folks that we should go to the backyard before they start something at the spot, but little did we know that death was in the backyard waiting for us. Once we got to the backyard things started getting really

13

hot. Bullets rang out while the BD's had the whole backyard surrounded shooting at everything in sight, I hit the ground, waited for a few seconds then jumped up and busted through the back door for cover. One of the folks got down under a car and the other jumped through a little garage window. It was only the grace of God that no one got shot or hurt, things were out of control, hate and frustration filled the air, "oh my God" what's next. The police got there really fast, ready to take one of us to jail and if they would have found any weapons in the house everyone living in the house world have gone to jail. All the guns were in an outside hiding spot, all but one gun. God blessed us in a strange way, the police could not find it and it was right under their nose, laying right on the bed under a folded blanket. Then I knew that it was time for me to get out of Peoria and start over with a new life.

Later that week we had a meeting about what we needed to do. Who needed to leave town due to having families. The choice was made for me that I had to go back to Arkansas, now part of me wanted to stay and fight and the other part of me wanted to get back to my new son and the lady I loved.

AHH, back in Little Rock Arkansas, no more GD alerts and I could not wait to see my girlfriend and baby boy. I wanted to tell her everything but knowing what I knew, it was best to keep that lifestyle in Peoria.
Wow, she was so happy to see me and I felt the same way about her. I felt like I had a lot to make up to her being gone so long and not being there for her or going to her prom like she had gone with me to mine.

I was so dumb to go but I was young and had to learn things the hard way about leaving such a love alone. I also was happy to see my son for the first time words could not explain the way I felt, I was proud to be a daddy, but didn't have

14

a clue on how to be a father. I had a great man to mimic, my father, now he was always there for us and I loved him and my mother so much still to this day in spite of their differences. One thing I can really say about my father is he was a hard worker and I believe that is one of the greatest things that I took from my father's positive life. It was something I learned from his life to help me become a good father for my family. One of the things I got from my mother was her heart, I always felt like if I treat people how I want to be treated, that it will come back to me one day.

I believed if I put my trust in God, take my time in life, and listen to the right people. I would one day get this father thing down, Okay so my girlfriend and I continued to see each other knowing that we needed to find a house. Not long after my girl found us a house right next door to her, I couldn't understand how that worked out, but we moved right next door to them and she was literally the girl next door to me. Now that was fun. We snuck over to see each other all the time, talking all night, playing games that we both enjoyed. She would come and wake me up when she got off work; making funny sounds for me to sneak her up to my room it was so cool. I know, everything sounds so good, yes we had fights and problems, but I felt that no one could stop our love for each other. I felt our love was like the sun that would never stop shining, it was poetic. Now there was a type of fear that tried to come over me, I haven't spoken of this fear yet, but that is how fear is, it comes and goes when you least expect it. After seeing how my mother and father ended up, I always felt that it would happen to me. I then began to get afraid, not wanting this love to end; trying to find out what I needed to do, or what I could do to be the right man for her and how to make her happy

15

forever. I really didn't want our relationship to end up like my parents, but I always tried to think ahead and that is not always a good thing to do when you are living by faith. I'm not saying my parents' relationship was bad and I believed that they really loved each other very much. I also believe my father was a great man, who knew how to take care of my family, but he was human and almost let stress and negative things get him down and only God can keep you from acting out in a negative manner. I wanted to be like my father, but not so much like my father, so I prayed and waited; meaning I wanted the good parts of him, but not the bad parts of him. I stilled loved him no matter what I would love to be just half the man he is, fearless. I still had this fear haunting me and coping in a positive manner wasn't what I was used to. I started to drink and smoke more, thinking that I was going to die, thinking that the love of my life was going to leave me. I continued to love her, I continued to work on my mind and heart, I wanted to become a better man for her in the future. I know that I should have been praying, but when you are young you try to do things your way. After trying over and over to make myself feel like I was fixing the problem I realized that I can't do it on my own. I then prayed about our life, I prayed that we would be in the will of God and get out of life what he had for us. I told my girlfriend that I loved her and wanted to spend my life with her. I then asked her, while we were lying on the floor at my mothers' house if she would marry me, she said yes. Now that was the happiest day of my life because I believed that I was doing this life thing the right way. I wanted to marry her because I loved her, not as a business plan like people do now.

Wow, I felt like the air was blowing freely in the wind, this has to be the will of god, God said he that finds a good wife finds a good thing; for it is better to marry than to burn and I believed that she felt the same way about me. I felt we had a love that only

16

Kings demand, I felt we had a love that only Queens dream of, I felt we had a love that only angels give. It was clear to me she was my light in the dark, my moon over the pier, my love away from pain. Now I know that I was young but I always believed in God, thinking about positive things such as living right, living righteous and treating people the way I wanted to be treated. I was not afraid to try or fail in life, my only fear was 'would I be the right man for my wife when I got married?' Only time would tell so listen up it's going to get rough.

I began getting back into church because I knew if I didn't have God in my life or in my marriage that it would not last. I believe that just getting married is not going to keep you in the will of God, but you also have to give God all the praise and glory too no matter how hard it gets in your life. I continued to pray that God would bless us and that I would be the best husband anyone in the world. My lady began going to church with me and working on her soul, not for me but for her, because God is the only one that can give you true happiness and peace entering into a marriage. Now there was very little planning involved, but I just wanted to be with her forever no matter what type of fears continued to haunt me.

The time drew near, the pain and fear of defeat began to haunt me more and more, visions of me not being a good husband for her, visions of me letting my love down, visions of my love leaving me. That fear told me that my wife was going to leave me because I didn't have any money, it said I was not fun enough for her, or I wouldn't be a good husband and that I was going to beat her.

I prayed and prayed that God take this spirit of fear out of me, I didn't want to go into a marriage with fear, and what was I to do when the time for us to get married was around the corner. Then it happened, we got married, I felt it was beautiful because we were in love and being in love was half the battle, so I thought. Now it wasn't a big wedding at all, just a small wedding and a little reception at our small trailer home that God blessed us with all the way in the woods. I always felt that when it came to something so important, so loving, so time consuming in your life, that it is not about starting off with a big house and nice cars. It is about having a big heart for God and each other; being nice and treating each other with love and respect, that is what I felt would make things last, if both partners are willing to work together.

Chapter 2

(Real Faith)

We didn't have much, but I felt that we could make it if we had faith and kept God in our marriage. She was working at the time, doing what she could around the house, smiling and making me feel that she wanted to be with me. She took care of a lot of the bills and I felt that was a blessing in itself because a lot of women would not do such a thing in the beginning of a marriage.

My wife was praying and letting God lead her heart and mind; she cooked and cleaned the house with a positive mind set on life. I felt that my wife was a very strong woman; she loved me and did not let anyone talk me down. My wife took care of everything that was needed to be taking care of in and out of the house. I was so happy to be married to such a woman of God. I was going to barber school at the time. I really wanted to help more with the bills, due to me feeling that it was my job and I wanted to free her from doing so much. I had some clients where I would cut their hair every weekend, it helped, because our bills weren't high. God really blessed us, with our rent being 150.00 dollars a month and the remaining bills came out to around 150.00 dollars a month.   My mother gave us a car so I didn't complain about anything, now I wasn't happy about everything, and I felt that I had enough faith to make a lie come true. I was so in love and felt that God would work everything out in due time. Over time, while out at our trailer home, I noticed that my wife wasn't smiling as much around me. She wanted to stay away from the house more, didn't want me to hold her as much nor did she want to have relations with me as much.

I was not feeling down as much as I would have before, I just felt that I needed to work harder at home so she would not have to work as hard. I know that it was hard for her to live so far out, but God blessed us with this home and I knew if we hung in there God would bless us with a bigger home.

It was getting harder to deal with, very little money coming into the home, not being able to take her out to eat or to the movies like I wanted to. So after a while I began to feel like I let her down. I tried, I prayed, I worked, I loved, I believed, but I just couldn't make her happy. My faith in God kept me staying positive with my wife. I know it was hard for her being married at the age of 19 and just as hard for me being married at the age of 21. But not long after that my wife asked me to leave and told me she did not want me anymore. I was crushed my heart was broken and my love was lost. My mother moved to another house, not right next door but it was fairly close to my wife's mother's house. So naturally I moved to my mother's house. Feeling like my life was over and the thing I feared the most happened to me. Wow, I could not believe my wife was done with me. Days later I heard a noise outside, thinking my wife was coming to see me and maybe she wanted me back. So I jumped up with joy, feeling like I could not wait to see my love again and with a big smile on my face I went outside, but the next thing I saw ripped my heart right out of my body.

I watched as my wife's mother and her little brother put my bed that my mother gave us and all of my things in the middle of my mother's drive way. I was hurt, I felt that I didn't deserve this treatment I had never hurt my wife this way, I only loved her and tried to be the best man that I could for her, due to being so young.

I know that I'm Christ- like but sometimes things can bring the devil out of you. I began to talk with my mother about everything, feeling myself getting in an evil mode. I was ready to say or do something stupid, but I knew that wasn't a Godly love and God let me know to forgive them, for they didn't know what they were doing.

So I prayed about it and continued to forgive them because I knew that if I didn't forgive them it would stop me from being happy. Remember if you don't forgive, then God will not forgive you and that will hinder you from growing in life.

I felt it was clear that my wife's mother didn't think I was good enough for her and maybe I wasn't. I continued to talk with my mother about what it was that I could have done wrong and thinking about moving back to Peoria, Illinois to get away from the pain. Now I knew that the mob life was there along with my old folks, but I didn't care I just wanted to get her and that pain off my mind (Jesus help me). My mother then told me not to go back to Peoria, but to pray, have faith, and hold on. Let go and let God work it out, focus on your soul and being right for God.

God will work it out or work her out, God then put on my heart to go to

21

this park where I would go have prayer time such as walking around it seven times calling out Jesus, believing that he is going to make a way for me. I prayed more and more, fasting and believing God would heal my heart and fix my love.

God began to work in my life on all types of levels, healing my heart, teaching me how to forgive her and my enemies so I could come out of my trials faster. God is so good too, while I was blessed with a new job working security, now that's not much, but it was a blessing to be working and going to barber school.

I began to feel stronger with my love and did not want to hold my wife back or keep her from doing what she wanted to be in life. I called her, to let her know that I didn't want to live in sin; doing things that I couldn't handle in a fleshly mindset, such as committing adultery. Suggesting maybe we should just let this marriage go, because it's not healthy for either of us.

Not many days later my wife came over to my mother's house saying she was not feeling good, she then mentioned that she wanted to work out our marriage. After sometime past we didn't live in our trailer home anymore, we moved into my mother's house until God blessed us with a new home. I prayed and continued to believe God for a home, because it was getting hard dealing with the little space in my mother's house and we were also trying to have a baby.

Wow, what do you know, my wife became pregnant with my son little Lonnie the third, now I know God was going to bless us, because we needed space bad with my wife being pregnant and us getting custody of my oldest boy. Not long after that, God blessed us with a nice apartment in North Little Rock, Arkansas.

I tell you God is always on time, with our apartment being just the right size for us starting out a new family. My wife is pregnant, I'm working two jobs and taking care of my family, also I have my oldest boy with us. I couldn't have asked for a better feeling. I was doing the best I could with what I had and feeling like a real man. Conveniently, my wife could not work and I loved it because I loved taking care of my family.

Now I still had some fear, because I wanted to be a great man for my kids and an awesome husband for my wife. I battled with that fear daily, knowing God did not give us a spirit of fear but of a sound mind and heart if we believe for it. Not hearing 'it's going to be alright or you are a good man made it harder to believe in myself. Now I'm not saying that it was my wife's fault that I thought that way, she just didn't know, or want to learn how to give me the type of support I needed from her, to help me believe in her. In spite of all that I knew that I wasn't going to fail and I wouldn't quit on my family, thanks be to God. So my youngest son was born and I felt like a king, with the biggest castle in the land and I had two princes with one queen. Praying was one of the only things that I knew, so praying is what I did. I began praying that God blessed us with a new home that we can call our own. Keep in mind that you must have faith and wait on God to move in your life. If you move too fast, or lean to your own understanding, you may miss what God has for you. God continued to bless me and my family with money, with food, and the right people around us to be a blessing to us. I ended up meeting a man that I can now call a friend, he had his own mortgage company. He and I began working on my credit and seeing what I could do to get my family in a house and out of that apartment. I didn't know how it was going to happen with me being the only one working, without credit, very little money, and my wife taking care of our two boys. So I did what I knew how to do, yep you guessed it, pray, because I believed that God would be there for us no matter what and he would supply all of our needs. Six months later, I asked my wife to look for a house because He had blessed us to buy a house.

Wow our first house, the favor of God and faith is better than money, if you ask me, but you have to believe or it will never work out for you. Now it wasn't a big house castle-like, but it was our home and I was taught that if you take care of the little things, God will make you ruler over many. That means be grateful for what God has given to you in order to receive more from God.

I was feeling good at this time my fear was not there, although it did try me at times with my job, my kids, and you guessed it, my wife. I felt safe when my wife and I prayed and let God handle our problems. Now this was a very important thing for us to continue to be positive with each other, it was a must; talking to each other, which was a need and loving one another, which is self explanatory. I felt like my wife was happy, she smiled all the time and made love to me without reason. I felt like our love was strong, it wasn't perfect, but who has a perfect relationship? If you find one just let me know, I would love to talk with them.

Now this does not mean that you can't strive to make your relationship perfect, but if you believe and follow the rules that God has for us in our marriage it could be perfect in a God's way, or at least you would have as many complaints with each other. I did wish that I could do more for my wife. I knew that she liked to have nice things but I just couldn't provide her with the finer things of this world. I saw in her eyes that she wanted more, I new she liked to shop and

24

go out and have fun with her family. So I tried to let her have her space, I tried to buy things for her if I could, I was there if she wanted to hold onto me and I was there to hold her whenever she wanted me to.

I couldn't give her much but I knew one thing that I could give her; all the love and honor in the world and if that wasn't enough, then I didn't know what I would do. I really loved my wife and kids and I would do whatever I could to make them happy with me and happy with their lives.

We were happy and living good, God had blessed me with another job and that would make three of them; being a full time father and a full time husband loving every minute of it. I was so in love with my wife and happy with my family, but I still had that fear haunting me, telling me that my wife still wasn't happy and she had made a mistake marrying me. So I continued to pray and believe in God, fighting with my mind, choosing not to notice or believe that certain things began to change, such as very little love making, very little holding and very little communication.

'Oh Lord, what did I do Lord, where did I go wrong Lord, help me Jesus, make me feel better Lord; help me be the man that you want me to be, help me to be that right man for my wife Lord, create in me the wisdom to know how to love my wife, forgive me for not loving the way that I should, help me be a great husband to my wife Lord, in Jesus name I pray Amen.'

Chapter 3

(The Turning Point)

Poems of life

☹

Like every real man I felt like it was all my fault and I needed to do more for my wife and kids. I began to love and listen more. I tried to show her more of my feelings by hanging around her more doing what I needed to do, to make her happy. I began writing poems about her and telling her I loved her more, but something was wrong because she still showed me no real feelings. She did not read into my poems like I wanted her to. I continued to write, because it helped me express my feelings to her and it also helped me release some of my stress. After awhile I started to feel like I was putting her before God, she became a distraction to me and what God had for us. She didn't know if she just wanted something better and I started to feel more and more that it wasn't me. One poem I wrote to her was called soul tampering.

Soul Tampering

Dear God, thank you for my life

Thank you for my soul

Give me the words to enlighten another's control

My soul is intrigued from the talk of the century

As her soft sweet voice embraces my feelings

My mind drifts to a land undamaged

I'm unable to manage

The joy that has been poured into my heart

My cup is overflowing

I can't spill a sip

Even if I have to get a sponge

For every dip

Soul Tampering

I will absorb her soothing emotions

Saturate my spirit with her sweet interference

My lady you are the flesh of my flesh

Bones of my bones

God is my witness

I'll do what it takes to keep her at home

Or in my den

But sometimes God will give my life a trim

For trying to put her over him

Lord forgive me for that sin

I gave her that poem and she just looked at it and said it was nice, now that wasn't wrong I just set my goal too high and thought she would read how my heart craved for her love and heart. I didn't know what I was doing wrong I only knew how to love or hate and I choose to love her and my family.

I continued to thank God and believe he would keep us happy because we wrestle not against flesh and blood but against spiritual wickedness in high places, now I told my self that all the time, but I didn't really know what it meant to the fullest just yet, But I would soon find out. She continued to look down and sad it looked like she was so unhappy my heart was in tears but I never showed her that. I just work on me and doing what I could to make her smile. Then she let me know that I was overwhelming her, she didn't say it in a mean way but it really did hurt.

Now how am I suppose to deal with this I was raised on trying to treat my wife with love and respect and to try to work out all my problems if we could, but I was too young for that kind of statement. I couldn't come up with any ideas on how to make this lady love me the way I loved her. I then made a mistake I let the unwilling side of my mind take me to another state of thinking which had me praying less and thinking more in a fleshly theory. Now I know thinking on my own is not allowing God to be a part of my life or living, but I was getting weak and needed prayer from my spouse.

Trapped

Society has me trapped
But who's the blame
Sickness and death is driving me insane
As my body is in pain
I wonder
Will I be able too endure the chains of strain
In a hole
To weak to get out
I need prayer and strength from my spouse
While mothers are crying
And brothers are dying
Pray for me
The world is hard
Hearts are scarred
While Satan sits back
Laughs and grin
Saying to him I know I'm going to win
Fear not

The battle is not yours
For Satan has already been defeated
God will give Satan the pain that's needed
So there's no reason to act demanding
No reason to whine
For the peace that passes on
All understanding will guard your heart and mind through Christ Jesus.

Now I loved to write, it was my way out of the world, but I started to stop talking to her as much, I stopped trying to hold her as much; I stopped believing in our love. See I began to think if I started living my old life again, such as speaking when being spoken to and thinking more about me and caring less about us then I wouldn't be hurt as much in my marriage.

She began to hang out with her family more, we didn't pray together at all really, not that we prayed all the time together but it was more then not at all. Our life became complex, such as no more love making, no more anticipating each others touch. I couldn't cope I was living a lie I wanted to hold her, but I felt she didn't want to be held by me. Some men might say that I was being soft but if they really want to know the truth that might be just be what your lady needs to keep her from cheating on you, so don't think its soft to want to hold you lady do it and if she refuses it. God will move it one way or another. Now as I was saying I began getting upset asking Jesus what should I do with this vivid defiant behavior hunting me, taunting me, telling me to snap and give up I tried talking to her but I really didn't get an answer out of her, maybe it was me I didn't know.

Answer me

Another day I can't sleep
My dream is trying to eat at me
Pain from mystery and unbelief
Why won't she believe me?
Why does she mislead me?
Why at night she loves me, but in light she hates me
Why do I always have something to write about, but nothing to say?
Why, is my heart broke?
Why is my love starting to float?
Why can't she love me for me?
Why won't she ever believe me?
(Jesus, please make it stop)
Why is the devil trying to make her leave?
                                Answer me

Why is the devil trying to make me bleed?
Why is the devil trying to make us disagree?
Why does she think she is the only on in pain?
Why does she dislike my frame?
Why does she feel like she is the only one that can change?
Why won't she just talk to me?
Why does she treat me like I was the one who took it G?
Can you feel me?
Why doesn't she trust her man?
Why doesn't she call her man a man?
Why does she think I'm a joke?
Why doesn't she believe I love her like a yoke that can't be broke?
How come I'm talking, but no one can here me/
Will someone please answer me!

But they were just words to her, so my distractions began to haunt me more. My fear began to test me; I felt my love stopped loving me. The anticipation mortified me. Complex behavior was upon me and coping wasn't a choice anymore. Jesus, help me, keep me from getting into the trap that the devil has set before me.

So I began mentoring the young men across the street from my house .Teaching them positive things and how to deal with some problems they might face in the future. Now I was taught that iron sharpens iron, but I was the only iron and no one was there to sharpen me. I prayed and made some mistakes but helping others around me helped me deal with what I was missing in my home such as family, honor, friendship, and positive conversations.

I still loved my wife, I still wanted to hold my wife, I still wanted to talk to her. But as a young husband who loved his wife, but did not receive that feeling back I was lost and did not know what to do. But I was haunted with a thought, how was I going to feel holding someone that told me that I overwhelmed her. So I didn't and every time I touched her I felt like a fool. We began to live an off beat marriage like two bands playing at the same time. Yep you guest it I started hanging out some meeting friends and talking to them about my life.

Now that was the dumbest thing you can ever do is talk to people about your relationship who are not giving you any spiritual word. Most people have all of your answers to your life and their life is a living mess. One of the number one reasons people break up in a relationship is from our lack of listening to God and our spouse.

People will lie to you and tell you they know what you are going through just to make you live like them, in misery. They are so unhappy with their life or don't really know about their life, the words they give you to them is the truth and that goes to show how the blind lead the blind right to a brick wall lost and lonely. Which is the exact opposite of iron- sharpening- iron. I still prayed and asked God to keep me from doing wrong, but I am human and I have made mistakes that were dumb, but I know one thing I loved my wife and really wanted to make her happy.

But I felt that she didn't care so why should I. Maybe I should do what I want to do maybe I should start hanging out more. Giving up felt right and taking control of all my thoughts is a thing of the past.

One More Day

Giving up is what I did.

Living a lie is what we did.

They say seeing is believing,

But I say believing is seeing.

Dreaming is what I love to do.

Knowing is how I like to feel,

But time waits for no man.

Maintaining is a thing of the past.

One More Day

It's all about you

It's all about what you can do for you

Where, is the love?

Where, is the life?

Where, is the loyalty?

Where, is the wisdom?

Where, is the knowledge?

When will we try to understand?

Living and learning sounds good, but what's living if you never learn. How will you ever grow, how will you ever love, how will you ever know what is real. Giving up sounds easy, but it is really the hardest thing to do.

Chapter 4

(Wise or Why not)

So I began doing just what the devil wanted me to do, such as not praying as much not believing in my wife, not staying strong like I was raised to, now for a young black man who wants to do right, but feels that his wife is not giving her all will start to take a big toll on your mind and heart. It could have just been me thinking to hard I just know that if you love someone it doesn't take a dam to break just to show you love them and want to make your marriage work.

So why not do what I want to do, who is it going to hurt, she is not showing that she cares and I'm tired of waiting for her to care. I then began to drink again not much but just enough to make me feel some peace, or so I thought. I didn't really go to the club as much I just hung out with my little buddies across the street. I always had ideas going on my head and when I talked with my little buddy a car stereo shop sounded good, so I started a shop called the Corporate Connection.

I did it all there from sales of clothing, installing car stereos, rim sales for cars and trucks, and mentoring the young men in my neighborhood. Showing them how to install car audio and how they can own their own business. My heart went out to young people whose parents weren't really in their lives. My boys were too young at the time to work on cars with me.   I did things with them, but not as much as I could do with them when they get older. But that doesn't mean that you can't love your kids and spend time with them at home or be a part of their school. I did provide a safe home for them, I loved them, I played with them, I also knew that when they got older I would be able to have more fun with them, but that did not stop me from trying to be the best father in my family's life. I felt like working all those jobs and having hobbies would keep the old me from coming out and acting like a fool.

Now maybe I should have tried harder to communicate with her and at the time I felt that I did but what did I know I was just in love and dumb. I then began hearing from a negative source that my wife was having an affair on me and not being faithful to me. I chose not to believe them, because when you start looking for something it is a proven fact that your mind will find something whether it is right or wrong and I don't care what anyone tells you, because if you are looking for wrong then wrong is what you will find.

I also believe if you bring or keep negativity up all the time then negative things will happen. So I continued to work and maintain a positive attitude as I could, considering how we have been getting into negative altercations. But we all know that if you give the devil an inch he will take a mile and that is just what he did. One of my wife's family members boyfriend at that time came to me during a family function saying that I know that you are a good man and trying to do the best you can for your family. I then said what is on you mind Joe, tell me what you are thinking, he then told me that your wife is cheating on you. I was mortified, but did not overreact on this negative statement. So I told him to wait and went inside the house to get my wife and I ask this man to tell me what he said about my wife cheating on me and he then without any hesitation denied it. Right then I chose not to believe it although we hadn't been making love for awhile.

Now keep in mind if you don't want to live in pain don't allow pain in you heart, yes I know sometime you can't help it. Pain always seems to find away into your heart but that doesn't mean that you should help it out. Long story short about pain just let go and let God take care of your feelings even though part of you might want to handle your pain in your own way.

I must say though that I felt that I wasn't in the will of God to do all the trials that I have been going through from fighting with my wife all the time, not working out our problems together and not talking or praying together at all. I began talking to more people in the neighborhood, hanging around the wrong people, hearing the wrong people and not feeding my spirit with positive information.

Now after several months of fixing up cars, moving clothing, and doing car shows something happen that woke me up and put me into "kill someone mode". I was sitting on my couch minding my own business watching television and I heard a loud bump. As the sound was going forth I looked at my front door and noticed that the middle was pushed in with a foot size hole in it. So without hesitation I jumped up ran to my bedroom to get my gun and then I noticed that since my kids were young I had put it up in one of my shoe boxes now that sounds cool but I had about 40 pair of shoes and the gun was in one of them I just forgot which one.

I started to toss shoe boxes everywhere telling my wife to get down and keep the sword with her until I came. After making a big mess I found my gun with one in the chamber aiming right at the door saying to myself if anyone comes through that door they are dying tonight. I then called the police and my brother Bozo, at that time was living in Arkansas also.

The police got there and didn't do much or say much just told me next time "wait, until they come in and shoot them". Now that wasn't what I expected from the law but to tell you the truth I didn't think they would have made it over to the house anyway after the police left my brother came with his ridiculously big pit bull named AK. Then my brother and I went outside to check around the house because the police didn't and noticed a nine millimeter shell on the ground by the front steps. God watched over us, no one got hurt and I didn't have to kill anyone that night. That incident made me think more about the safety of my family. We were on high alert I slept by the front door for a week, I walked around with a gun; I stopped talking to my neighbors and told my wife to start looking for a new house. I felt like everyone was a suspect and the first one that comes to me or my family wrong will get the business. Now I'm not trying to be a tough guy, but I will defend my family by any means necessary.

My wife and I were getting along do to all the drama that was going on, but I didn't know how long that was going to last. Nevertheless she started looking for a new home for us, God blessed us in the midst of our troubles and we were able to refinance our home so we would be able to fix our credit and move to a new home with a good interest rate. All my wife had to do was find us a home.

Now I was ready to move but when listening to the wrong people it tend to make you question if you are doing what is right, such as going through drama and disagreements, do I really want to move into a new house with my wife. I chose yes because I am a fighter and I will continue to fight until God says it is over.

We looked at some nice homes but two were very nice and we really tried to get one of them but God had other plans and that was alright with me I just wanted my family safe. We continued to try and the deal didn't go through and I began to get frustrated, but as my mother would say sometimes you just have to stand and wait on the lord. In the mean time my soul was getting sick of the neighborhood and everyone that came passed my house were starting to look guilty I am not cool and still walking around with my gun.

I knew that God didn't like this behavior out of me, but I am human, so I prayed with my gun on my hip. One day I was just looking in a home magazine and noticed that a great deal came right before my eyes, well it seem to be cool to me judging from how we were living which was also blessed I might add. But that is just how God is he may not come when you want it, but if you believe and hold on God will be right their whenever you need Him.

I saw a 2200 square foot ranch style home with 5 acres and a stocked fishing pond on it. It was 3 bedrooms, 2 ½ bathrooms a large den, big kitchen/ dining room and two car garage, which could be all ours. It wasn't far it was in Jacksonville, Arkansas and it sounded like something my brothers and I use to talk about when we were kids. I told my wife about it thinking that she would feel the same way about the house. She said "I don't know", not in a mean way she just wasn't feeling it like me, but she did say we could go look at it. We drove to Jacksonville to the house after it snowed and when we pulled up I felt like I was in heaven, wow, a beautiful house with a two car garage, and flat land with a clean blanket of snow over it. The water in the pond was sparkling like clear stars, or like a pair of beautiful eyes.

The look in her eyes just wasn't right, she new I loved the house, but it wasn't just for me it was for my family I just wanted them safe. Now the other homes she picked out didn't work out but I was for them all I asked that we try this one out. I wanted to stand in the kitchen one time and that would tell me if this house was for us. The reason for that statement is I had a dream that I was standing in this big house right in the middle of the kitchen and I felt happy. Now that could just be me but I felt I had enough faith to make a lie come true and I wanted my family out of that neighborhood. Yes I went back and walked in the kitchen and felt the presence of God all over me, yes! This is it, but will my wife agree?

She didn't agree and I felt bad because I just knew that this house was for us so I prayed about it, and ask my family to pray about it feeling that this was the right move for my family. My brother Jimmy, our realtor and I went out to the house and prayed in the back yard asking God if it is his will to move and work things out for us. When I got back home my wife and I talked about it again and she then said okay, but she did not want to live there no longer the seven years.

Chapter 5

(Unyoked **Move)**

Move in order

Nightmares of me waking up in a puddle of tears
Fearing the past
Hunted by the future
Will I make it?
Can I take it?
Sick of being tested on my love
Tired of being rejected about my love
Profiting and interjecting wisdom from above
The peace that passes on all understanding has
Forgotten me
Leaving me
Where is my peace
Should I move?
Should I live confused?
Yokes are meant to be strong
Songs are meant to be passed on
Unyoked moves are doomed to begin with a grin
But in the end it just leaves you lost and living in sin.

Wow I heard what she said, but it seems to me that thanking God was in order, since

someone tried to kick our door in and possibly tried to rob and kill us. I didn't let it get to

me I understood what she was trying to say I just wanted us to be on the same page with

this move.

I talked with her about some of my dreams for our family hoping that a spark

would arise in her. I didn't want to move with her unhappy, but I also had to think about

the safety of my family and me not having to kill anyone for trying to break into my

house again. She then started to show some life in our move, she started to look for

furniture and pictures to decorate our new home.

The lord continued to bless and work out our move. It was happening so fast I

just couldn't keep up with how fast God was moving for us. That is why I say you have

to wait and trust in God and he will take all your troubles away if you allow him to. I

couldn't of asked for a better transition, we got help on our move, beautiful furniture,

nice cars such as Mercedes Benz, jaguar, and custom suburban. Now I am not trying to brag, but God had been blessing us so much, such as, a blessed move and stable jobs.

I felt good, but my wife still had that look in her eyes like she just wasn't feeling this move in the right way. Now what do I do? How strong is my faith for this next move? Help me oh Lord, help me to be strong and wise to your word, help me to listen to your guidance for my family, help me to see what you want me to see not what I want to see in Jesus name I pray amen.

Thank you Lord, I love our new home, it is so nice and roomy, and we have so much space. God has truly blessed us and my wife was a pretty good decorator, she had good taste in furniture. I felt good about that, it made me feel that she really did like the home God blessed us with. Now I don't care how much you fix up a house, without the real love of God flowing within both of you it will always look good on the outside but ugly on the inside. Now she did work on being up under me, showing me love and making love to me and that helped me stay on task with my feelings and having more faith in believing that she was happy with the move and happy with me.

Keep in mind she was never a bad mother, she loved both of our boys and did whatever she could to make them not want for anything. But I still felt deep down inside that she wanted to be happy with me, but did not believe she could be happy with me. I don't know maybe it was me; I am not perfect and have not been strong for her like I know I should have. But what I did know was, I was trying to make her happy the best way that I knew how in this life time. After a while she began to have that look in her eyes again, they were filled with pain, loneliness, stress, and hopelessness in me or in anything I tried. But like I said before maybe it was me, maybe I didn't know how to be a good husband or a good father, maybe I should have let her live her life, maybe I shouldn't have asked her to marry me, maybe I took her life from her, maybe I just needed her to show me love the way God showed us. Maybe I wasn't sexy enough for her; maybe my faith wasn't strong enough for both of us. Maybe this move was the wrong thing to do, maybe I failed her.

Now this is what I felt like every time I looked into her eyes and after we moved in our new house. Now was my faith being controlled by my fear or did my fears take control of my tears? I felt so bad, I felt I wasn't being a strong man, my poems began to get darker, my heart began to get harder and my soul began to get meaner what was I to do? My wife didn't communicate well with me at all. I don't think she didn't want to, I just think she didn't have the faith to let God teach her how to listen to Him and her husband. I began to grieve my love for her, I felt my love was starting to deceive me, but giving up was not the answer so I began to find ways to occupy my time in a positive way such as working out and lifting weights hard, becoming stronger preparing my body for combat.

I wanted to play football in the AFL,(Arena Football League) which was an indoor pro football League they paid a little money, but it wasn't about the money I just wanted to try something I have never done before. So I brought this dream to her to see if she would support it and she and her mother just laughed at me. After that they became my fuel, I felt like I was a joke to them. I felt like negative

46

feedback was a beautiful thing it made me grow mentally, physically and spiritually.

I went to the AFL to try out and I did very well, so well that they brought me in as a prospect for the next football season. Now I wasn't able to play that season since I had not played football before, but I had the faith and the heart to do anything. But a week later I got a phone call from a coach that was over a semi- pro football team and he told me that one of his players saw me at the try outs and recommended me to come to his try out that was coming up soon. I then went to that try out and did very well there also and not long after that I decided to be a part of the team called the Arkansas Rhinos a NAFL which was a semi- pro football team. I knew that was going to be hard to do, having a family and two boys, but I felt it would also give us something to do together as far as going to the games and supporting me. So practice began with the team and I had to pick my boys up from school then go to practices. My practices were on Mondays and Wednesdays and I was coaching my boys on their football team on Tuesday and Thursday when their football season started. This went on for about four years going out of town playing football and coaching football with my boy's team, but this only went on during the football seasons. Now she showed support for our boy's no question about that, but I don't think she really cared about me playing football at all. So to keep myself occupied, not thinking about whether or not if my wife loved me I began to work security at a night club. It was hard to do from working full time, playing football, coaching, and being a good husband and father, what was I to do, I was overwhelmed and did not want to be, but it kept my mind off everything. The love and respect that I craved at home was not at home it was in everything else I was around. So yes with God not running my house I'm doing what I wanted to do and she's doing what she wanted to do we were doomed for only on thing to happen.   But you couldn't tell me anything I felt no matter what I did from giving her half of the money I don't have, after working security at the club she still was going to do her thing. Now I was wrong for working in the club without talking to her about it, but if you wanted me to talk to you about what I was doing then you should talk to me about what your doing. I was sick of being a good person and showing so much love and respect for nothing. By this time I had made a few friends do to me not really having anyone to hang out with, I felt it made life a little easier for me when dealing with confrontations. Now keep in mind God was not in our relationship like he was at first. I expected things to look right, but are very much wrong and that was something that I had to learn the hard way since I wasn't listening to the holy spirit. Our marriage was being ripped apart and we are the only ones that were to blame, now that was something that we were going to learn the hard way. Yes it was on, and I really didn't care about my marriage anymore. I gave up on love and gave up on my wife making love to me, but as much as I wanted to cheat at that time my heart was constantly being convicted, so I got on a compliment high.

Now this is a very deadly thing for your relationship it is very easy to fall in love with it if you are not getting compliments at home. Although I wasn't cheating I craved the compliments that women gave me and by not getting them at home it made that need for attention grow.

Okay now this is real and a lot of men might lie about this, but most men are more insecure then women we just can hide it better such as having a lot of ladies, big nice cars knowing we can afford them, or making you, the women believe in homemade conversational statements that don't mean anything to us just to make you, the women say one thing, you are a good man. Okay let me show you what I mean, now when a real man, with real feelings tries anything he doesn't really get noticed by you, the women at all therefore, making his positive fight on deception harder to deal with. But on the other hand a man that is a whore, doesn't care about being a father and will sleep with every woman he looks at gets praised and talked about which only helps him not fight deception, but becomes deception itself, praise is praise whether it is good or bad, it just ups the receiver of the praise and what level he wants to be on after he receives his praise, which makes a man handle his own insecurity as a man than as a God fearing man. In a nutshell positive praise brings positive men and negative praise brings negative men. Okay know back to the story, I loved receiving praises and the more my wife didn't do it the more a random lady would. So the more I coached, played football, worked, worked out and fathered my boys, the more I felt like a man outside of my home not inside of the place I lived. To me a home is a home when home lives in your heart and it doesn't matter how big your house is or how much money you have.

Now I continued hanging out more, craving praises, craving a peaceful conversation, wanting to communicate with my wife but it wasn't in her she said, "She doesn't talk well." Now ladies if you feel this is not one of your strong points in your life pray that God will teach you how to communicate, because in the end it will come back on you, but like I said this was my problem and I have to learn how to let my faith run my life not run my fear.

Now when I talked with people I didn't lie to them. I would always tell the truth about my life and my goals, not knowing it was like a verbal attraction to them. Then right after that the positive praises came like it was imperative that they give me one as if they felt they were going to get a blessing for being obedient. I didn't know that this behavior of mine was driving her to a point of no return, for example she planned a series of negative behavior that was joined to our madness, and at this time negative was that last thing our relationship needed. I knew that this was going on, but couldn't understand how we would allow this lust for power, hate, and self control take control of our lives. We played right into the devils game, I set things up, I made things up, I even did things that I wasn't proud of, I was so arrogant and stupid I told her if she was looking for something I would make sure she found something. This became our life no love, no trust, no sex, no belief, and no God. This was a very confusing time for us. I couldn't understand how my wife would give me so much attention when I stepped out of the will of God, but when I was in the will of God she didn't speak to me as much, she didn't make love to me as much and she showed me very little attention. I am not saying that she was a bad women, we both needed to grow up, but you have to notice your wrongs first in order to grow from them, you not only have to talk about treating a person right you have to be about treating that person right. Love them like, God loves you that is a good place to start if you don't know.

I was so depressed from all this playing, I didn't believe in myself or my marriage. My depression drove me to a suicide mind set with the gun in my hand, not because she didn't give me her love, it was because I was sick of my love for her. I was sick of feeling like a loser on the inside, I was sick of taking care of a family that didn't notice me, I felt like I was worthless to her why should I continue to fight for a myth.

I went to church because I didn't know who I could run to, or who would make me feel better as a man. So I prayed and cried that God would help me work out this pain with or without her, part of me wanted to stay with her, but the other part wanted her gone because I knew she was not happy with her life or with me. But like a fool after talking with her about getting a divorce and planning what we were going to do I let deception sneak into my mind. I met a young lady who said all the right things but at all the wrong times, I was a bigger fool for believing in this woman and I knew that I still wanted my wife. I let the devil tell me that this girl could be the one for me, I was so blind I let my pain get fed daily by this deception, but what was I to do or say, my wife didn't want me she was in and out of town doing her thing. Now there was no excuse for my actions I was taught better than that, I knew it was wrong even if she didn't or wasn't taught how to love unconditionally. I let this young lady know that I was taught better than this and I could no longer be a friend of hers, I let her know that I wanted to get back into the will of God, I told her I needed to do this thing right and if God ended it then it will be ended the right way. So after being convicted by God and not being proud of my sins I let God know that I wanted to be in his will and to help me be the man of God that he had chosen. So yes, I continued to go to church

51

praying and believing in doing the right thing for me. Asking God to teach me how to have more wisdom and understanding on how to deal with my old and new trials that I would face. But it seemed like the more I tried to make it right the more she worked against me or what I was trying to do in our relationship. There was a situation that I felt did not deserve the outburst that we displayed. There was a storm that was bad and it started a little water leak in our den, so I let her know that since it was a bad storm that our insurance should pay for something, instead of it coming out of our pocket for the work. Not only that I believed that I could fix it myself. So after that one day I came home from work and noticed that there was an insurance check in the mail. Now I didn't know that she call the insurance company or new that we were getting a check, but I was glad that she did. I then called my wife to let her know about the check and that I had a great idea that will help both of us out with past bills and new projects. I let her know that I fixed the leak for very little of money and I wanted her to hear out my plan. She then got upset with me and we got into a fight over the phone. I then got very angry knowing that my idea would work out for the both of us, but I was sick of fighting with my wife over little things. So I started to beat and punch the phone in a evil rage splitting my knuckle. I was sick of this life, I felt God let me down or have forgotten me. I began to drink vodka to relax my pain and depression. I waited on my wife to get home from work and she did not saying anything to me or not saying anything about my hand dripping blood she just sat there with a proud look on her face so I kicked the table over and went to the kitchen were I began to cry with hate, anger, and pain. She walked right past me with a cold blank look on her face not saying a word. Then she left and took my youngest son with her to where I believed was her mothers house.

I knew then that it was time to separate from this madness it had become very unhealthy for me. I talked with her about selling the house since she didn't like it or wanted to live there anyway. I was hurt but after living there for about five years neither one of us appeared to enjoy our lives in this home, Lord forgive me for that sin and not believing in you and allowing the devil to take control of my life and my thoughts.

**Chapter 6
(Healthy Pain)
Short and real**

I then contacted a realtor friend of mine to let her know that we were trying to sale our house and if she would help us with doing that. She said, (that she would love to help and feel free to let her know about any changes in the future.) Now I wanted to keep the house, because I loved it and she didn't, but she said her lawyer told her not to move and to stay there anyway. She stayed at the house, but did not want to help me out on any of the bills and I was sick of it. I couldn't take it anymore so I moved me and my oldest son to a town house in little rock and yes my youngest son was able to come off and on a little while later, so he too was able to be with us. I was able to take him to school after a month or so. Now all I had was a couch set, two fish tanks, a little single bed for my son, and a TV. She let me know that she paid for all the furniture and she was going to keep it, I felt like if she felt that way then cool she could keep it I will just trust in God for all my needs and wants. So I did and moved everything I had by myself and I continued to thank God for blessing me to move with very little money and very little furniture and I was going to continue to let God lead me. No I'm not perfect and I am no saint, I did hang out some and I had fun with my friends it was a whole lot of fun but in a nut-shell I felt peace. I did want to try to work things out with my wife, but the more I think about what I went through I began to harden my heart and chose not to call her. She did call me saying that she wanted to come home and I had hardened my heart, saying to her "we don't have a home it's up for sale and you didn't want it anyway." My fear wouldn't let me believe her, so I waited and continued to take care of my boys; yes they were with me most of the time because I took them to school and picked them up from school. Now don't get me wrong she helped with them, she also picked them up at times and she was still a good mother.

I know you've heard the phrase when it rains it pours, well friends it started to come down on me. My mother was down visiting and going to look after my sister's kids when she went on vacation and when they got back they discussed with my mother about going to apply for her social security at the federal building and doing so my mother was beaten up by the security guards. Her tooth was knocked out of her mouth, her face was bruised all over and her arms and legs were bruised too. I was able to see this because my mother's sister called me while I was at work and as soon as she said what happened I was there in a flash. After I got there all I could think about was breaking their necks with my bare hands so I could feel there bones snap, but I knew that would have made me worse and I wasn't a gangster anymore. I then took a deep breath and let God guide me on what to say and do. So my mother had to go to the hospital to get formally checked out and to make sure she was okay emotionally. My mother had to stay with my sister for two months and then she had to come live with me due to some miscommunication

56

problems. So now I was looking after my mother and taking care of my two boys believing that God was going to work out everything for us. This went on for about a year and during that time my wife and I tried to work things out again and it was harder because we didn't trust each other for nothing. I prayed and I'm sure she prayed to, but I'm sorry actions speak louder then words and if you want to make something work you have to do something to make it work. So if you say you love someone, show it and if you say you believe in someone then believe in them or keep your dreams selling to your self. I still felt that she wanted out and if she didn't want to be on her own then she would do whatever it takes to make it work and not think about self.

For example, I didn't want us to go out of town anymore without each other because we needed to build trust and love for each other through hanging out together and praying together. But she felt that she was going to do what she wanted to do anyway, so she started to plan a trip to Arizona with her friend who lives there and I felt that it would be cool as long as I could go, I thought it would be nice to get away from everything for a weekend. She gave me a disturbing look after I asked her about going saying, "yea you can go softly under her voice." I knew then I wasn't a part of that trip or a part of any fun that would go on in Arizona. When it came time for the trip she let me know that she didn't want me to go with her, now what do you think went on in my mind? I didn't feed that negative energy that was trying to come out in me I just continued to let God lead me and stay focused and peaceful. I then asked her in a calm manner if she would not go on this trip and to wait for another time so we both could go on a trip together. She let me know that she was going anyway and would I take her to the airport, I said, "No I would not be a part of this and would not speak with her during the trip at all." So I didn't speak with her because I felt I was a big joke to her and I knew that the devil wanted me to get upset and start hanging out again, but I didn't, I continued to pray for peace in my soul. That Sunday night God put on my heart to pray for my wife and for her to have a safe trip back, and I told God no I didn't feel she was worthy of them, I told God I didn't care if her plane fell out of the sky. I told God that I'm not going to be hurt by her again; I was tired of this double minded spirit. I knew that this behavior wasn't God's love and I needed to obey God no matter what, so I prayed for her safety and for her to be kept from any hurt, harm, or danger.

After she got back and called me I decided to pick up my phone to talk with her, she let me know that the first plane she was on was struck by lightening and they had to wait for another plane. She then let me know that the other plane had to be placed on hold due to malfunctions. I told her that I believe that is why God had me praying for you to have a safe trip back. I told her that I didn't want to pray for her and she should thank God for humbling my spirit to be obedient. I didn't know what God was doing, but I knew that I wanted to be in the will of God and I needed to stay focused on what he could do in my life as a young man. My wife and I continued to work on our marriage, such as talking about getting another place together. I felt that this was good for us, talking more about getting a place, but she made it clear that she didn't want to buy another home. I felt with that statement she really didn't plan on living in Arkansas long, but I said nothing I just wanted to see where God was going with this.

She then talked with me about her having some problems with her body and how she is always sleepy, no energy and having mood swings. I let her know that she needed to go get checked out to make sure that everything was okay and if there was a problem that she needed to fix it before it is too late. So we went to the doctor and were told that she did have some problems that would need to be taken care of and for us to start setting up arrangements that were comfortable for her to live in. So we did and I felt that it was a good way for her to see how much I really wanted to make her happy and to show her that I had her back during this hard time. I felt like this was not a mistake and to continue to let God lead me that way I will not feel bad if she decided not to be with me, so maintaining and staying positive was a must for me during this time.

Chapter 7
No trust, No forgiveness, No progress
(Right to the point)

I believe that a mistake is not a mistake if you learn from it, in my book it is called a learning experience, but when your mistake becomes a repeated mistake it is not just a mistake, but a negative outcome in your past history and you are doomed to repeat it, due to lack of processing mistake building skills. .

So, I asked her if she wanted to try again and if she would like me to find us a three bedroom apartment for us and my mother to live in for now. I let her know that I would be there during her surgery and after her surgery so she could have a nice place to sleep. She looked at me then with a sad look on her face and said that she would take a chance with me. Wow, she said she will take a chance, I felt this is where people that wanted God to work out their problems need to get an understanding on.

Okay the word chance means something that happens unpredictably without discernible human intention or observable cases, and the word faith means belief and trust in and loyalty to God, believing and trusting in him. This is saying that when you are going to take a chance, you are saying there is room for doubt and doubt comes with confusion and confusion is not of God.

So after she said she would take a chance, I knew that I would have to pray harder and continue to have faith on this move. The move was made and not long after that she had her surgery. Yes, I was right there with her before the surgery, during the surgery, and after the surgery. I was at the hospital holding her hand praying that everything would be okay for her and when it was time for her to leave the hospital I had a three bedroom apartment with her furniture in it waiting for her to come home. I tried to make her feel as comfortable and as safe as I could, from helping her to the restroom and getting food for her whatever she wanted me to do I was going to do my best at it. She then asked her little cousin to come over and help her around the house and take her places when she needed to go somewhere, now I believe that was a good thing, because her little cousin can be a really strong successful woman of God if she believes and lets God lead her. So she started to move around more not really needing my help with getting up or laying down, she started to drive around and even began to pick up things on her own. Yes, you guessed it after a while she began to get that look again as if she made the wrong choice something was holding her down, the sad part was I felt it was me. We didn't really become that close during her healing process in fact we might have grew apart more, when I asked her was she still in love with me, she said no.

Wow, now how was I to deal with that statement, I am not in love with you anymore, and to add wood to the fire she had planned to go on a trip to California without me not even fully healed from her surgery yet. No she wasn't mean when she said it and I don't think she wanted to hurt me, but pain is what I received from it. So she was off again and I called her to try and make her see that I was the real deal, from saying I was sorry and letting her know that I really wanted to make things work, but she really wasn't feeling me she sounded so far away mentally, physically, and emotionally. Yes I continued to pray for her and us that God would work things out the way he wanted to work things out not the way I wanted them to work out. I felt this was coming to an end, but I kept the faith, and knew that God would guide me on what to do, because I don't believe she really took me seriously at all, as a man or as a husband. So I was led to write her a letter about my feelings and how I would like to be in her life.

The Letter

Hey I wanted to say first I wish that I could have been the man of your dreams. I'm sorry that you fell out of love with me. I believe you are the best thing that happened to me. I thank God everyday for you, and what I been through with you, I wish that you would tell me how to love you or what kind of love that I can give you to make you happy. I tried to be the best man for you, I know this is hard for you and I know you love me, but I just don't know how to make you smile. You have so much fun with everyone but me. You smile and feel so good when you are not around me. It hurts me so much when you don't have fun with me, I feel like I lost the war. I don't know why I made you feel so bad, I hate myself for that. You are so lovely and pretty with the sexiest lips. I want to understand you. I want to learn all about you again, teach me how to love you the way you wanted to be loved. I love you and it makes my soul bleed knowing that you are not happy with your life I want to listen to you and learn how you think.

It went something like that, but after I wrote that letter I began to feel that when she got back from her trip that she wouldn't be the same. I called her a lot due to missing her, but didn't talk to her as much since she was not picking up the phone.

63

I began thinking that the marriage might be over, or this marriage might have been over for a long time I just didn't know it. I prayed and then started to gather peace and rest in God's word that no matter what he will take care of me and heal my heart from pain and confusion. I also let God know that I was going to trust in him, forgive her, and believe that when she came back God would help me be humble to her and listen to his guidance on what to do and when to do it. I believe that if I do God's will and obey God I will have peace whether she chooses to work it out with me or leave me. The time came and she made it back safely, I had balloons and flowers waiting for her, not to impress her but to make her feel at home. I believed she liked it so I then gave her the letter as I was on my knees so eagerly waiting on a response. Wow, complete silence in the room, I believe she felt it, but I don't think she wanted my love anymore, her face was without an expression, her eyes were white and plain, and all I could hear was her tell me "don't cry". But the spirit of God kept me humble, saying to me fear not for I will comfort thee my son. Not long after that I came across some pictures that I really didn't feel at peace with so I calmly called my wife to meet with her about them. She told me that the picture didn't mean anything and she wasn't trying to hurt me, so God put on my heart to ask her again if she was still out of love with me and was she ready to be on her own and her answer was yes.

Days after that she began to smile and feel better like she got so much pain off her chest, she was talking more and trying to interact with me more. I couldn't understand it, but I knew this is what she had been wanting for a long time. So I asked her how long did she think God was going to allow her to treat me like this, she then ask me what did I mean, I told her this behavior that you are displaying is confusing and not right if you don't want to be with me why are you here with me. She then moved out and went back to her brother's house. God put it on my heart that it was time for me to move and I needed to move when he said move. So after about a week I let her know that my older son and I will be moving to Tulsa, Oklahoma out of obedience to God and me wanting to do the right thing I asked her if she and my younger son would move with us so we can start all over again. She said with authority "I am not moving to Oklahoma". After that statement she told me a story about when she was in Oklahoma at a women's encounter that God told her that if she didn't move to Oklahoma that she would lose her house and her family, so what was her choice?

Chapter 8
Faith and Obedience

This is a love story, but sometimes love stories are sad with sad endings, I prayed that this was not a sad ending. It is funny how people want true love and spend half of their life looking for it and when they feel that they don't have it they are unhappy. I feel that people who are looking for love should ask themselves, do I need love or do I want love? It is hard for you too love with all your heart, if you do not love yourself first. I believe you will always be lost and unhappy because you wouldn't know real love if it was to bite you on your face. **(I also know that the beginning of knowledge is to fear God and no one fears God anymore they just think that they are God's themselves, fools are what they are.)** Okay my point is fear God it's the best way to love yourself and God will teach you how to love, then he will send you someone to love.

Now after being obedient and believing that God would supply all my needs I started to travel back and forth from Arkansas to Oklahoma not knowing where we where going to live, where I was going to work or what school my son would even go to. I just continued to let God lead me on this move, so I put out my résumé with some connections that God had blessed my brother to have, who I might add owns one of the top cleaning company's called Q tips cleaning in Tulsa, Oklahoma. I was able to be blessed to meet an extraordinary women, who at this time was like a second mother and was able to help me get approved for my condominium in less than a week. I had very little money and very little time since my lease was about to be up in that three bedroom apartment that I got for my family. I just continued to let God lead me and my move in his order and in his time. I went to my oldest son's school to make sure all his paperwork would be in order because I knew this would be a rough move for him as well. I also talked with his mother who I might add stepped up with a positive statement and said if she had custody of our son she would have let him move to Oklahoma with his father anyway because a young man really needs a real man to teach him how to be a man. All I could say was may God bless her and her family for being obedient.

The time was drawing near and I didn't have any furniture or a bed to sleep on. I only had what I started with when I moved to my townhouse which was a single bed, two fish tanks and a TV. But not once did I doubt God, I kept on believing that God would work it out for me on this move. God then blessed a friend of mine to call me right out of the blue, who had no idea that I was moving to ask me if I needed any furniture, because he had some for sale. He told me that he had a couch set that was in great condition that I could get from him for $100.00. On top of that he told me that I could pay him whenever I was able to. So I picked up the couches from his house and began to load my truck with whatever I could. The first trip was not so bad. The weather was nice and I didn't have any problems on the highway, it was a safe and humble trip that God blessed me to make. On the second trip that I took to Oklahoma I did the same as far as loading my truck with the rest of my furniture, but there was a little problem with the weather. There was a very bad storm that I had to drive through it was horrible, I couldn't see, I couldn't drive fast, a four hour trip took me six hours to get to where I needed to be. I continued to pray and fight through that storm. Now my third trip was coming up and not only that, time was crunching down on me.

I had a job interview that I had to make on time, and on top of that there was a test that I had to pass that I hadn't studied for. I had to pass it if I wanted to work at the job that I wanted. This was a nationwide test that is required to be passed if I wanted to work in the school system. Now for the people who know me know that I hate taking tests and I hate studying for them, but I had faith and trusted that God would bless me to pass this test and I also believed that if I do the possible that God will do the impossible. That night God put into my spirit and reminded me that about five years ago I took this test when I was working for the school district in the state of Arkansas and was to check my score that next morning.

That morning I made the call to find out my score for the test that I had taken, and it was a 455 and the passing score was 457 in the state of Arkansas. Then God had me to check to see what Oklahoma's passing score was, and their passing score was 455. Wow, look at God, I had no idea that the test I took five years ago would be just what I needed to work after I moved to Oklahoma.

Now I know that this is going to be tough, but I had to stay focused for my boy's, and also show them to trust in God not man, because man will let you down. I wanted to teach them to always move with faith in God and not to ever let it turn into a chance, to always believe in God and his promise on their lives.

Now after properly preparing for this transition it was time for me to move my mother, my oldest son, and I to our new home in Tulsa, Oklahoma. So I loaded up my Escalade and began a new walk in a different direction with the same God.

The move went very smooth for us I wasn't able to work at the school yet due to waiting on some paper work. I was able to work in my brother's clothing store called Two Brothers Clothing which has some of the cleanest apparel that you will find in Tulsa Oklahoma. I didn't have to worry about my looks because my sister kept my hair fly, who I believe is the best hair stylist in Tulsa, Oklahoma. She has her own salon in the Promenade Mall called His and hers salon. God has really been blessing me in this new walk.

I know that it is not going to be easy, but it is a lot more peaceful giving everything to God and not fighting everyday, and I am learning to give my problems over to Jesus whether it is mental, physical, or emotional and I know if I have faith in God and trust in his word my transition will continue to bloom. After about a month more of our transition continued to work out, my oldest son was doing well in school, making good grades, playing on the football team and is one of their top athletes. My brother and I worked out a program where we can help my mother with her living arrangement. I became one of the coaches at my older son's school working with him on the football team. Our closets were full of clothing and shoes, and I was on time with my bills and rent at my condominium.

I just want to thank God for being there for me and placing the right people in my life, at the right time in my life. I want to thank God for taking care of my mother and my youngest son and his mother while going through these troubled times, I want to thank God for my sisters and brothers for listening to God and letting him lead them to be a blessing in our lives also, I just ask that God will continue to make me be what he wants me to be and not what I want to be, I pray in Jesus name that this book helps and guides other couples to do the right thing and to be obedient to God and what he has them do in Jesus name I pray amen.

Chapter 9

My belief in relationships

First of all I would like to say women are beautiful and the world would be lost without them. This is not a section about tearing women down or breaking their hearts. I would like to openly express my mind, if I may without causing tension in your relationship.

Okay we have all heard the words men are dogs, but what we really should say is people have commitment problems. The majority of men and women that are called dogs have had their feelings ripped, emotions crushed, and hearts burned to a degree of no return. I would like to download a few tips that may help keep your feelings from getting mangled in your relationship.

TIP 1

You should always be honest and up front about your relationship, and what you want out of your relationship.

TIP 2

What you did to get that person, you need to keep doing it to keep that person.

TIP 3

Don't be afraid to admit when you are wrong about something in your relationship.

TIP 4

Do what it takes to please your significant other in the bedroom

<u>TIP 5</u>

Always leave room for failure, so you have room to grow.

<u>TIP 6</u>

The most important tip of all is always trust in God, because he will help you trust your mate.

If you apply my tips or learn how to apply my tips to your relationship, you would feel

better about the choices you make with your mate.

The second thing I would like to discuss is self-esteem. Your self-esteem is so

important and deep in your relationship you would need a dictionary to understand it. For

example, if I don't take care of body I am depriving my spouse of her visual pleasure that

she deserves. If I don't build up my mind I am depriving her of conversation. Most of all

if I don't build up me, I am depriving her of me.

I have been through a lot of ups and a lot of downs, and I have found out that most of our bad situations are not what they seem and most of our good situations are how we allow our minds to perceive them. Everyone would like to be in a relationship without drama, but no one wants to put up with the drama. Now listen to me closely. If you want your relationship to be successful, you have to fail first.

For example, if I'm in love, but don't know how to love, then I would enter a relationship with false love which will cause my relationship to become an unforgivable love. Therefore in order for me to become the man that she loves I would have to learn the proper way to love so I can be loved.

In conclusion, I would like to talk about the most important tip of all. This tip doesn't need a long drawn out word because God is the word and without Him all would be lost, and I believe by having God in your relationship and believing He will work out your problems, and that is a beautiful thing to know.

I believe if you are having problems in your relationship that the first thing you should do is a complete overhaul of your life, you should find out where you are with God and develop a personal relationship with God. The second thing you should do is talk with you life partner, and both parties should write down their negative and positive thoughts that need to be worked on, and all the mental thoughts that you would like your life partner to work on. The third thing you and your partner should do is write down all your physical problems and physical goals that you would like to over come with or without your life partner. The forth thing both parties should do is write down all your emotional ups and downs that you have experienced in your life.

I believe that these are mandatory points that you and your life partner should have done in the beginning, or should do in the beginning, because it will teach you how to communicate with each other with an open heart, and you would know up front if there are any secrets that need to be addressed. It will also teach you how to not accept, but love each others personal and self-esteem mishaps that they have been dealing with all of their lives.

I believe that you should develop a personal prayer time with God, and then develop a prayer time that you and your life partner can pray together, make it fun and real it shouldn't feel like work just love, believe and do it. If you don't know what to pray about pray that God will help your relationship become whole, pray for mental, physical, and emotional strength in your marriage, hold each others hands when you pray.

I feel that marriage is a personal ministry that every married couple should want to please God in. I learned this the hard way, but if we are seeking God with all our hearts he would put into you the spirit of love and how to love unconditionally. Treat your life partner how you want to be treated, hug them, kiss them, look at them, and talk to them like it is the last time you will ever see them. No one knows when they are going to die, it could be today; stop neglecting yourself from real love. Love as God loves you, don't think if they are treating you wrong or lying to you, don't go looking for problems, put that misleading spirit in Gods hands, because it will bring you and your love down. Let God deal with them, it might be a learning experience that they are going to need God to get them out of, just pray that they come out of it alive mentally, physically, and emotionally for you, and if they don't let God guide you where you need to be in your life.

What I am trying to say is let us start using more common sense when it comes to loving one another, there are to many politics involved in our marriages. We only care about what we can get, how we can get it, and when it's over, what can I take with me, so I can be okay.

Next, say something nice to your life partner, don't be afraid or to cold hearted make them feel special, don't let your pride keep you lonely and unable to forgive, and please don't be afraid to be creative or accept creativeness in the bedroom, stop deceiving yourself you need to have a healthy and spiritual sex life, trust me.

In my conclusion I just want to thank God for my trials and battles that I over came, and for the humble heart to learn from them. I want to thank God for teaching me how to listen and how to be obedience to his word, because I feel we are all like children in this thing we call love, sometimes we all want to do good like a child, but you still have to have adult supervision.

YES, God did bless her and my younger son to move to Oklahoma, so look out for part to A Dream Without a Song (Where Do We Go From Here).
I just want to say put God first,
 Keep God in the middle,
  And let God end it.

**Chapter 10
(My thoughts)**

Love for all Saints

Condemned by the blind
So many saints are unable to look past there grief
So filled with mystery and unbelief
How dare we say we believe in God but question his seed!
How dare we say we trust in God but won't let him lead!
How dare we live in this world without faith!
We pray for that
We pray for this
But when God starts to bless us we treat it like mist
I'm hurt
I feel like an eclipse covering the land
So sick of fake people stealing our joy
Playing us like a toy
We are unable to grow

We are unable to smile
We are unable to try
We are unable thrive
We are unable to live faithful lives
Spending all our time in places we don't need to be
Listing to people with no faith and very little belief
Why do we question Gods plan for us?
Why do we question Gods love for us?
Let go saints and let God take control
Trust in God and the connections he places in your life
Be committed.
I love and trust God
 I believe in his word
I am to loyal and focused
To lose and be hopeless

Don't put love and lust
Together, for love will grow

And lust will just go away
— — — — — — — — — — — — — — — — — —

People listen to what they

Want to hear, and don't hear

What they need to listen to

Think before every decision,

Because it might be your last

- - - - - - - - - - - - - - -

A bad situation is only

A blessing in progress

Having faith is the first
Step to becoming a man

- - - - - - - - - - - -

Books too look out for by Lonnie c Edwards Jr.

Other books available online @
Food for your mind (God help us all): Amason.com &
www.createspace.com/3779851
Resurrected Demon Compressed & Defeated: Amason.com &
www.createspace.com/3779927

Books not available yet, but coming soon: **The Adolescent in Man**

Mental questions

Emotional questions

Religious questions

Notes

Notes

Notes

Printed in Great Britain
by Amazon

80390054R00052